EXTREME

sports

skateboarding

W
FRANKLIN WATTS
LONDON·SYDNEY

contents

Skateboarding has been around for a long time. The idea of the skateboard came from surfers in California in the 1960s. They wanted to try 'surfing' on the dry land.

In the 1970s skaters mainly rode their boards in parks made specially for them.

Then, skaters took their boards out onto the streets. They turned cities into huge playgrounds where they could try out their skills.

Skateboarding is one of the most exciting sports around and more and more people are getting into it. This books shows you how you can join them.

what is skateboarding?

Skateboarding is hard to describe. It's not an ordinary sport. There are no rules, no teams, no competition. Skating is a way of testing your skill and courage. It can be anything you want it to be – a pastime, a fun method of transport, even a way of life.

The great thing about skating is that it's enjoyed by people all over the world. Wherever you go, there will be new places to skate and new skaters to ride with.

Skateboarding can change the way you look at where you live. It allows you to find pleasure and challenge in places that most people ignore.

5

the board

Deck
The deck is the top of the board. It is made of wood. It's covered with special tape to help your feet grip.

Trucks
The two trucks connect the wheels to the deck. They contain the hangers, the base plates, the rubber cushions and the king pins.

Wheels
The wheels are made from a tough plastic to stop them wearing out.

King pins
When you turn these large bolts they change the turning speed of the trucks.

Wheel bearings
Each wheel has eight metal bearings to make it spin.

Hangers
The hangers hold the wheel axles.

Rubber cushions
These allow the trucks to turn smoothly. If you change the type of cushions it will change the turning speed of the trucks.

Axles
The wheels turn on these metal rods.

Base plates
These connect the trucks to the deck.

where to skate

There are two main types of place you can skate –

- the streets
- and skateboard ramps.

Street skaters ride objects in the streets such as curbs and walls. This tests their skills.

Ramps come in different sizes
from mini ramps to huge verts
(see pages 30-31).

learning to skate

Skateboarding is not something that can be taught. There are no rules telling you what to do or which tricks to learn. Just look at the pictures in this book, watch other skaters and, most importantly, stick with it.

Most cities have somewhere where you can meet other skaters and learn new things from different people.

Don't worry if you find it difficult to start with. Part of the thrill of skating is that it is a challenge.

Even the experts had to start somewhere. Most of them have been skating for many years to get this good .....

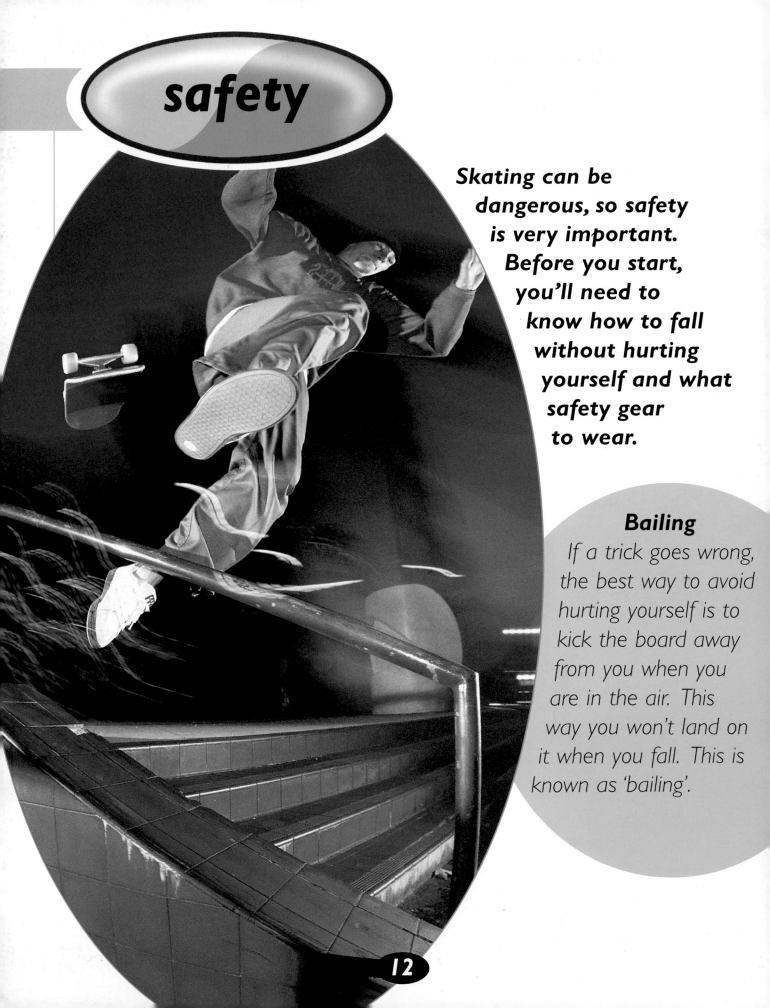

safety

Skating can be dangerous, so safety is very important. Before you start, you'll need to know how to fall without hurting yourself and what safety gear to wear.

Bailing

If a trick goes wrong, the best way to avoid hurting yourself is to kick the board away from you when you are in the air. This way you won't land on it when you fall. This is known as 'bailing'.

Pads and helmets

All skaters should wear hard pads and helmets to protect themselves.

started

Before trying any of the tricks that you'll see in this book, it is important to get used to riding your skateboard. The two basic skills any rider needs are –

balance
and board control.

Pushing

Practise pushing along on flat ground until you feel ready to stand on your board.

1 *Put your front foot on the board.*

2 *Push yourself along with your other foot.*

3 *Put your other foot on the board once you're moving.*

To stop, just put your back foot down again.

Carving

When you feel happy just going in a straight line, you're ready to start turning the board.

Turning or 'carving' on a skateboard is simple. Just lean towards the direction that you want to move in.

Lean back a little on your heels to turn the board in that direction.

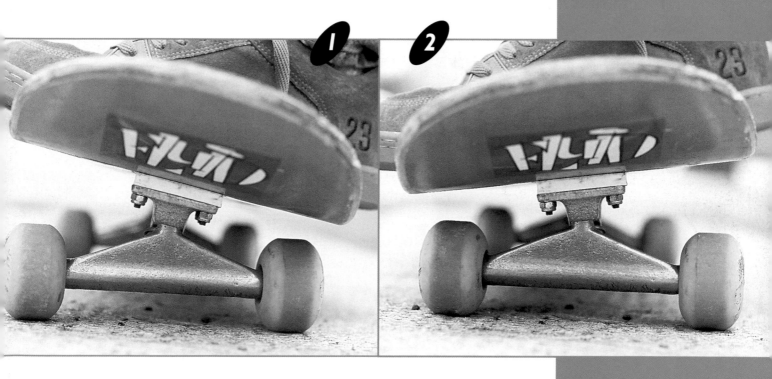

Lean towards your toes to turn your board the other way.

Keep practising. It may feel strange at first but it will start to feel natural after a while.

frontside and backside

'Frontside' and 'backside' means the way a rider is facing. The words were used by surfers to describe how they rode waves. If a surfer were facing the wave when he did a trick, this was known as a frontside move.
If he were riding a wave with his back to it, it was a backside move.
These words are also used in skating.

All moves and tricks can be done frontside and backside. If you learn how to move on both sides it will mean you can do many more things on a board and you will be a more complete rider.

A frontside move.
The rider is facing the ramp as he makes the jump.

This picture shows a backside move. *The rider is facing away from the ramp.*

the ollie

Once you've got the basics, you're ready to start learning some tricks. The ollie is the first move to learn. It's a simple jump which you should know before going on to more difficult tricks.

1

2

3

Tips: *The ollie can be tricky to learn. Try it when standing still at first. Once that feels comfortable, try it when you are moving. Don't worry about how high you go. The more you practise, the higher you will be able to jump. You can use the ollie to jump over just about anything!*

1 *Put your back foot on the tail (back) of your board. Put your front foot on the middle of the deck.*

2 *Crouch down slightly. Imagine yourself in the air.*

3 *This is all about timing. Lift yourself upwards. As you do this, push the tail against the floor with your back foot. As soon as you feel it hit the floor, lean towards your front foot. Your front foot should now be guiding the board upwards.*

4 *Pull your knees up towards your chest. Try to get the board straight beneath your feet.*

5 *Crouch down slightly as you land. This will make the landing smoother. Ride away happy and smiling.*

19

ollie grab

This trick is a type of ollie. You hold the board with one hand when you're at the highest point of the jump.

An ollie grab will help you to control your board when you are in the air. Try one when you're jumping off something high or riding a ramp.

A grab allows you to turn more easily in the air. This means you can try different tricks with less danger of losing control of your board.

There are many different types of grab. They have different names according to which hand is used and which part of the board is grabbed. We can't list them all here, but the pictures should give you some idea.

Tip: Make sure you can do the basic ollie before you try a grab.

flip-tricks

Flip-tricks are like ollies, except you flip your board over when you are in the air. There's loads of different types of flip-trick. The kick-flip is one of the easiest.

1

2

3

The kick-flip

Start as if you were going to do an ollie.
Crouch down.

Start to lift yourself upwards. Push the tail of your
board towards the floor with your back foot.

When the tail hits the ground, kick your front
foot upwards and out. This will flip the
board over.

When the board is the right way up, try to
catch it with your back foot. Then put your front
foot down on the board.

Crouch down slightly when you land.

skateboard parks today

Skate parks today are very different to the parks of the 1970s. This is because skateboarding has changed so much. Street skating has become more popular and riders can now do many more tricks than before. Today's parks are a mixture of ramps and objects like those found on the streets.

grinds

Skating on an object by grinding along is one of the most difficult moves. Skaters slide along the object on one or both of the trucks of their board. Grinds are a great way of testing your board control.

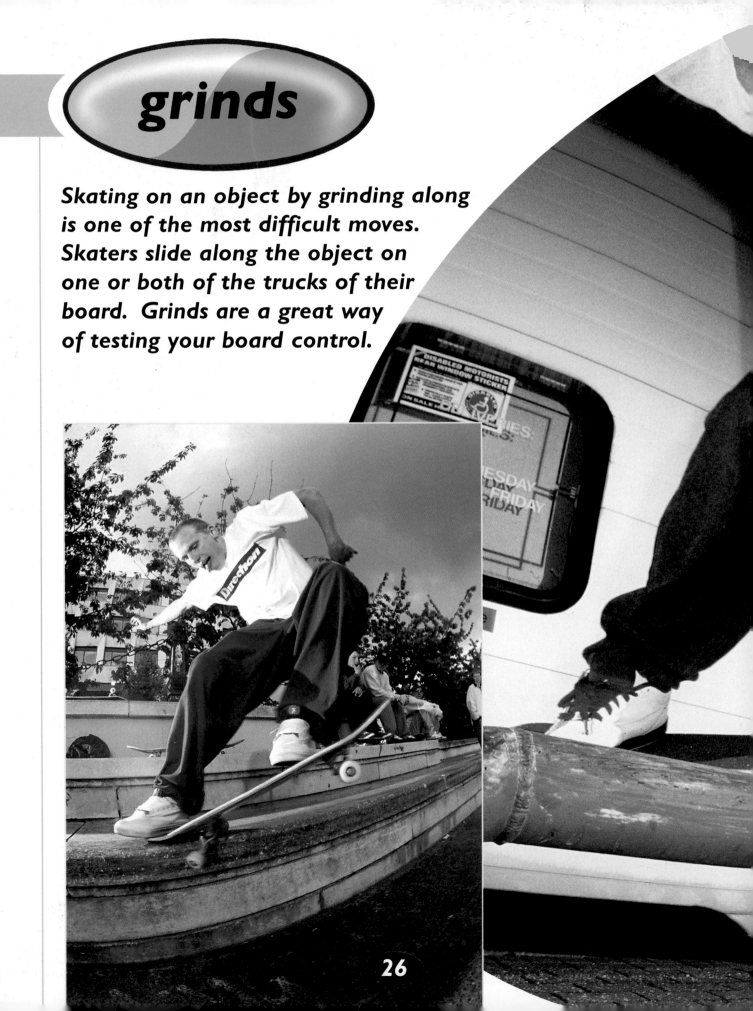

Grinds can be done on almost anything
– like steps, rails and ramps. The faster
you're going when you jump on the
object, the longer you will grind.

Some things are easier to grind than
others. It is easier to grind on metal
than stone because it is smoother.

handrails

There's no limit to what can be used by street skaters. You can skate on just about anything if you practise – curbs, steps, walls . . . and handrails.

Handrails are probably the hardest objects to skate. They're certainly one of the most dangerous.

Handrails are a real test of your board control. Leave them to the experts.

vert ramps

Vert ramps are the largest and steepest of all skateboard ramps. From the top of the ramp it's a sheer drop into the ramp's curve. It's best to start off on smaller ramps before you switch to vert.

The height and steepness of vert ramps means that riders can travel at amazing speeds. The size of vert ramps makes even the most simple trick feel good. Imagine grinding on a four metre vert ramp at top speed. It's a great feeling.

extra stuff

Disclaimer

In the preparation of this book all due care has been exercised with regard to the activities depicted. The Publishers regret that they can accept no liability for any loss or injury sustained.

Text: Ben Powell   *Series editor: Matthew Parselle*
Photos: Wig Worland   *Art director: Robert Walster*
Designer: Andy Stagg   *Reading consultant: Frances James*

This edition published in 2000 by Franklin Watts
© Franklin Watts 1997
Franklin Watts   *Franklin Watts Australia*
96 Leonard Street   *14 Mars Road*
London EC2A 4RH   *Lane Cove NSW 2066*
A CIP catalogue for this   *Dewey classification: 796.2*
book is available from   *ISBN 0 7496 2773 5 (Hb)*
the British Library   *0 7496 3609 2 (Pb)*
Printed in Dubai

Useful Contacts

A4 Distribution
Tel: 01925 757999

Bondi Boards & Blades
(Australia)
Tel: 02 9365 6555

Index